THE PAPER IT'S WRITTEN ON

THE PAPER IT'S WRITTEN ON

Defining your relationship with an editing client

Karin Cather
and
Dick Margulis

&/ ✦ Andslash Books ✦ New Haven ✦ 2018

The Paper It's Written On
Defining your relationship with an editing client

By Karin Cather and Dick Margulis

Published by Andslash Books, New Haven, Connecticut 06515
www.andslash.com
sales@andslash.com

© 2018 Karin Cather and Dick Margulis

Disclaimers: This book does not constitute legal advice. This book does not create an attorney–client relationship between you and anyone else. When in doubt, you should seek your own legal counsel. A contract creates legal rights and responsibilities between parties, so consider running your contract by a local lawyer.

ISBN: 978-1726073295 trade paperback

Second printing

Design and composition: www.dmargulis.com

MANUFACTURED IN THE UNITED STATES OF AMERICA

*To our clients,
whose unforeseen situations and behaviors
continue to inspire refinements
in the contracts we write for the next time.*

THE AUTHORS

Karin Cather (www.catheredit.com) is a former litigator. She has been a freelance editor, the owner of Karin Cather Editorial Services LLC, since October 2014. Karin edits academic works, law, memoirs, police procedurals, science fiction, thrillers, true crime, urban fantasy, and literary fiction.

Dick Margulis (www.dmargulis.com) is an experienced editor and book designer who has specialized since 2004 in helping authors be their own publishers.

CONTENTS

Preface	ix
It's Business	3
The Basics	10
Kinds of Contracts	14
Great Expectations	16
The Anatomy of a Contract	17
Remedies	39
Dissertations	43
Other People's Contracts	46
Conclusion	51
Appendix: Sample Contracts	52

PREFACE

THIS BRIEF BOOK GREW out of a presentation we gave at the 2017 Communication Central conference, in Rochester, New York. We are grateful to Ruth Thaler-Carter, the host and organizer of that conference, for providing the opportunity.

Many people who have excellent credentials as professionals in the publishing industry find themselves at some point working for themselves. At first they may not think of themselves as being businesspersons, but they eventually realize that they are in fact running a business and that there's more to it than just being good at editing.

This theme plays out every day on mailing lists, in Facebook groups, and in other venues. Someone encounters a problem and wonders how to avoid a repeat of the same problem. Often the answer comes down to adding a specific clause to their contract. Sometimes it's just realizing that having a written contract is an essential part of a business relationship in the first place.

This isn't a law textbook. It's a resource to fill the gap between the generic small business advice available from SCORE or the Small Business Administration, none of which addresses the details of the publishing environment, and the specific but costly advice of a publishing attorney. You're a smart person who is good with words. You can use what you find here to draft a clear contract that works for your specific business and then, if you choose, pay a lawyer a modest amount to review it.

—DM and KC

THE PAPER IT'S WRITTEN ON

IT'S BUSINESS

CONTRACTS ARE A CONSTANT challenge for independent publishing workers. That category includes writers, editors, proofreaders, designers, project managers, and others involved in producing books, journals, online content, and other kinds of documents and media products.

This book discusses the who, what, when, where, why, and how of contracts with individual authors and other clients. The focus is on the relationship between editors and authors, because we're editors.

A contract defines your relationship with your client

You and your client are proposing to enter into a business relationship. You may or may not have other sorts of relationships with your client. Most clients start out as strangers. Many remain no more than cordial acquaintances. But your client may be a friend, a friend of a friend, an in-law, or a close blood relative. Those other relationships may be complicated, but all you want to define in a contract is a clear business relationship.

> **Business is business**
> Many years ago, my sister's apartment in New York was burglarized. Her jewelry was stolen. Some months later, she was visiting our mother in Cleveland and mentioned that she was invited to a formal event but had no jewelry

to wear. They went to the bank where our late paternal grandmother's jewelry was stored in a safe deposit box. The jewelry wasn't our mother's style (or my sister's, for that matter). But it had sentimental value for my sister, and she selected several pieces.

Driving home, my sister mentioned that she also needed shoes for the same affair.

"I have a pair in my closet that I bought on sale but I never wore. They might be just right."

Sure enough, they were perfect.

"That will be twenty-seven dollars, please."

My father overheard this. "Jayne, you just gave her thousands of dollars' worth of jewelry. Now you want to charge her twenty-seven dollars for the shoes?"

"The jewelry wasn't mine to sell. But I paid cash for those shoes. Business is business."

—DM

You are running an independent business. You may not have thought of it that way before. After all, you don't have employees. Your "office" may be one end of the dining room table that you clear off if company is coming. You may work in your pajamas. Maybe you don't even have a business website. Nonetheless, you are offering a service in exchange for payment. That's a business.

What that means is that whatever experience you've had in the past as an employee of some other business doesn't apply to your relationship with your client. Your client is not your boss. You are your own boss. You and your client are on an equal footing. You are not obligated to let the client dictate the terms of your relationship. It's the contract that dictates the terms of your relationship, and this book can help you make sure that you put the right terms in yours.

A contract aligns expectations

The project you and your client are entering into is more complicated than going to a store and buying a head of cabbage. You are going to be sending one or more files back and forth, with steps each of you is responsible for executing. Your judgment is involved. Your expertise is involved. Other people's schedules and deadlines are involved.

As an editor and an author talk about working together, questions arise, at least implicitly: What is the nature of the project? Who determines when something is good enough? How are you going to communicate? How much do you get paid, and when?

A contract answers these questions in a document that you both agree to. When you sign one, you both know what to expect. Avoiding unpleasant surprises is one of the main benefits of having a good contract.

A contract is a sales tool. It shows your prospective client that you understand the project and know how to complete it.

If you only think of a contract as a formal legal protection to use as a cudgel when you want to sue someone, you are missing most of the value of a contract. The most important thing a contract does for the parties is manage their expectations, which reduces the potential for conflict at all.

All kinds of things can go wrong in a business relationship, and a contract does provide some protection against those eventualities. But those should be the exceptional events. You may go many years or indeed an entire career without ever needing the protection a contract affords.

On the other hand, the positive aspects of the contract come into play week in and week out, in every project you do, because the contract keeps you and your client focused on the steps needed to reach a successful conclusion.

A contract can help your business finances

A contract is *commercial paper*. If your client is creditworthy, then the contract represents money that you anticipate receiving and that you can persuade someone else you will be receiving. That someone else may be an analyst in the commercial lending department of your bank, so that when you apply to the bank for a commercial line of credit, they'll look favorably on the idea of establishing one for you.

What does a line of credit do for you? A line of credit is money you can borrow with a mouse click to pay your current bills and then repay when your client pays you. If you are working on a major project, with payments that are due only every few months, a line of credit lets you stay on top of your day-to-day expenses.

To establish a line of credit, you have to show the bank that you have the means to repay it. You'll have your business records, of course, and your tax returns. But showing that you're a going concern by providing a handful of current contracts will also be a big help.

And if you have to send a debt to a collection agency, a contract is a lot more useful than a copy of an invoice that doesn't have a contract behind it.

Why have a contract?

Clients pay us to provide a service. We market our services to convince even more clients to pay us to provide a service. Most of the time, we successfully perform the service and get paid for it. Sometimes we don't. When a project doesn't go well, it's important for us to know our rights and responsibilities.

The easiest way to know what these are is by drafting a formal contract. Now, many of us don't call our contracts *contracts*. You may call it a *service agreement*, for example, or a *letter of agreement*, or a *state-*

ment of work, or a *memorandum of understanding*. Or you may just have a series of email messages that constitute a contract without any title other than the subject line you use for those messages. But for the purposes of this book, we are going to refer to these agreements as *contracts* because that's what the law is going to call them.

Wait, what?—the law? Am I going to court? Is there going to be litigation? Is not having a contract going to prevent litigation? Is this dangerous? Will there be yelling? Are you mad?

Having a contract doesn't mean that you have to sue a client who does not pay you, although later in this book we discuss why that might or might not be a good idea. In fact, a contract reduces—not eliminates—the likelihood that a business transaction you are a part of will result in a demand for a refund—or a lawsuit. A contract makes it easier for you to collect payment. But a contract isn't just a sword; it's a shield. It protects you in case someone demands money from you or sues you. If a client posts a negative review and complains that you didn't do work, and if that work was outside the scope of your contract, you have something to defend yourself with. (We'll talk about remedies later in the book.)

You might so hate confrontation that you would never dream of asking a client to pay you after you have sent an invoice. You might be upset, and you might have to eat ramen. Or you might not make your health insurance payment. But you would never, ever want to ask anything of a client. Maybe to you it's easier to walk away. And if the client decides that they want their money back, no matter how unreasonable the demand, perhaps you have decided that it's not worth it to insist on being paid, no matter how many hours you spent on a project. Maybe you walk away from hundreds or thousands of dollars all the time—or are prepared to.

But even if that's you, you need a contract, in case the client sues *you*—unless, of course, you plan to hand over all your assets to a stranger rather than fight back. There are some nasty people out there.

> **Note**
> This book is primarily about what to put in a contract that you write when you do business with an individual, including another sole proprietor. Larger entities—publishers and other corporations, universities, law offices, and similar—usually have their own contracts that they expect you to accept. Later in this book, we'll talk about what to watch out for and what you shouldn't sign without talking to a lawyer first.

You may think you don't need a contract with anyone. You have never had a problem with a client, and you don't know what all the fuss is about. Maybe you don't think of yourself as a business owner and have not thought of yourself as dealing with clients at arm's length. Maybe in your mind a client becomes part client and part friend—until they're not.

What could possibly go wrong?

As a businessperson, you have to look at a contract as a sales tool, something that gives your prospective client a good feeling about doing business with you, and a means to align expectations between you and your client so as to minimize the possibility of conflict.

On its face, it seems simple. Because you're an editor, you're promising to edit a writing. They're promising to pay you to do that. But your contract needs to be as specific as possible. In this book, you will learn about a number of ways in which your agreement could be misunderstood and about terms that you should put into a contract to avoid these misunderstandings—and maybe even to fend off the kinds of people who are looking forward to taking advantage of you.

What misunderstandings? What conflict? Most of the scenarios in the following pages have happened, and if you spend time where editors and other creative service providers gather, you will recognize them.

My friend/son/mother/colleague said you're a terrible editor

You have been retained to edit a 40,000-word dissertation for $x,x00. You have wisely arranged for payment in advance. You do your very best work and return the document on time. A few days later, you receive an angry email from the author.

A friend of theirs who likes to read a lot and finds errors in books and who has no editing education or training decided that you made all kinds of mistakes and did a terrible job. The author began several sentences with *and*, which, they say, is wrong. And you didn't change those. You have also left in place split infinitives, and you have not fixed sentences that end in prepositions. You stetted the sentence "You have another think coming," and the noneditor insists that it should have been "You have another *thing* coming." You put some language into the first person or in the active voice, but you left some sentences in the passive voice. The friend offered to re-edit their dissertation for $50 and a loaf of banana bread, and the author is now convinced that you have done a shoddy job and ripped them off in the process.

Now what? Suppose you tell them that you did the work properly and you gave them the edited dissertation, and you aren't giving them their money back, and so their father emails you. He's a lawyer, and he's going to destroy you, and you better give back every penny of that money.

Now now what?

2

THE BASICS

Elements of a Contract

You may have made a contract with someone in the course of email traffic. If the two of you have had an email conversation in writing that describes the project, the work you're agreeing to do, and your fee, it might not matter that it isn't all on pages with the word *contract* on the top. Generally speaking, a contract put on paper by itself is no different from an email chain that covers an offer, an acceptance, and consideration (what it is that each party gets out of the bargain).

> Laws differ between jurisdictions, and the outcome of a controversy may turn on a factual nuance, so you should definitely consult your friendly neighborhood lawyer about your particular case.
>
> —KC

The problem is that those email chains generally don't contain the kind of detail required to protect you from worst-case scenarios, and there may be an authentication problem, also known as I-didn't-send-that-itis. A contract

- includes an offer, an acceptance, and consideration
- requires a meeting of the minds
- must be clear enough on its face that an impartial but overworked and impatient third party can understand it.

Ambiguity is bad. Plain language is good.

A contract is a *writing* (a written document) that sets out an agreement between (for purposes of this book) two parties, each to perform their half of a bargain so that both can benefit. The contract sets out the rights and responsibilities of both of you. As such, it's there to protect both of you, too. It should tell someone who's never met either of you what's in it for both of you to engage in this particular transaction, what it is that you promised you were going to do for this client, and what you were going to get in return.

A contract allows for no oral explanations. If you imagine telling a decision-maker that what you meant was—, or what you thought they meant was—, or what you both discussed afterward, or what you meant to nail down later, it doesn't happen that way. Your client won't remember things the same way you do, and if they demand a refund because they believe that you messed up, they aren't going to agree on what you decided orally. What's more, if God forbid you end up in court over this, it is very likely that the court won't hear any testimony on what you two talked about, anyway, because evidence of the conversation is likely inadmissible. This is such an issue that it has its own name: the *parol evidence rule*.

Your lawyer in your jurisdiction might tell you something different, and that's fine. But why have to cover this particular issue with a lawyer at all when you can avoid the whole thing by having it all in writing?

Disputes between editor and client are not always because greedy, dishonest authors love taking advantage of financially vulnerable, naïve editors. Often, the problem is that both sides have a differing picture in their minds of what the transaction is all about. Yes, sometimes the relationship is complicated by officious intermeddlers and sometimes there are authors who think they have the right to take peoples' work without paying for it. Some authors just have so little respect for what editors actually *do* that they can't believe that anyone would ever actually pay for it in the first place.

To be fair, some people out there call themselves editors who have no education or training, formal or not, and so they collect money from authors for the privilege of making their manuscripts worse. Because editing is an unregulated profession—unlike, say, the law—anyone can say they're an editor, even if they don't know anything about the editing profession at all. A contract demonstrates for the client that at least the editor knows about scope of work and that all levels of editing do not look alike.

Why can't you just have an earnest conversation with the author over the phone and make sure that you two understand each other? Anyway, the author is a friend or a relative, and they're a nice person! Or they have been your client, like forever! What could possibly go wrong? Why be so formal? Why be so melodramatic!

Because people hear what they want to hear. Because financial reversals happen. Or people get sick. Or relations break down. Or clients find someone cheaper. Or people don't remember certain details. Or, or, or. And sometimes people really do want to cheat you, or they might feel entitled. Some people are bullies, so sometimes you might get taken advantage of. Conversely, maybe you weren't particularly clear that day, or the two of you were talking at cross-purposes.

You have told the author that their book sounds interesting and the author hears that you are promising to get their manuscript onto the New York Times Best Sellers List. You have given them an hourly rate that sounds eminently fair to the author and then sent them an invoice that makes their hair stand on end, because they think all you're going to do is run spell-check, and how long could that possibly take?

This book isn't intended to paint authors as venal monsters or editors as helpless victims. A lot of red-flag-ey people take off when you send them a contract, and most people are happy to have a document that shows that their expectations are aligned with yours.

Is it true that you can trust some people on a handshake? Yes. I have two individual clients who, if they don't pay me, I'll have to go outside and watch the flying pigs crash into the Four Horsemen of the Apocalypse. But they're the exception. Unless you are doing business with them, you need a writing.

—KC

So let's talk about what needs to go in one.

KINDS OF CONTRACTS

No matter what the title of the document says, a contract is a contract. Somewhere in the document, you might even include the words "this contract." But different business relationships are generally memorialized by contracts with different titles. Here are a few:

- *Proposal, service agreement,* and *statement of work* (SOW) are different titles for essentially the same document. It says what services you propose to provide and how you intend to charge for them. It may also include a project schedule. Once the client signifies acceptance by signing the document, it's a contract. This is the typical type of contract you would use for a project with a defined beginning and end.
- A *letter of agreement* (LOA) lists the services you can perform for the client and the rates for those services, but it is open-ended and not tied to a specific project. If you are providing ongoing services on an as-needed basis, your contract will likely be an LOA. An LOA may include a *retainer* as one of its provisions. This is a minimum monthly charge for being available to do a certain number of hours of work for the client whether or not that work is actually needed in a given month.
- A *memorandum of understanding* (MOU) is often an interim informal agreement to write a contract. It sets out the basic outlines of what you and your client have discussed and agreed to, with the details to be filled in later in a formal contract.

- A *service level agreement* (SLA) defines the level of service you are willing to provide. In other words, it sets out the business hours during which you will respond to the client; the speed with which you will turn around work of a known scale and scope; and the quality standard you will uphold. SLAs are probably seen most often in the software support business ("Our system will be available 99.97 percent of the time, and we'll respond to your support ticket within thirty minutes, twenty-four hours a day"). But an SLA would be just as appropriate for someone copyediting tweets for a corporate client. Take care in drafting it that you do not inadvertently turn yourself into your client's employee. If they set your hours, provide your software tools, and give you a computer and a place to sit, you might have trouble persuading the Internal Revenue Service that you're an independent contractor.

4

GREAT EXPECTATIONS

Most people are not villains. Much of the conflict that arises between parties to an agreement is the result of differing, but unstated, expectations. Contracts make expectations explicit for you and your client. But what if the client won't sign one?

Maybe you put expectations into a contract and the client doesn't like the boundaries you have set. Maybe the two of you renegotiate and come to an agreement that aligns your expectations and satisfies you both.

But maybe you send the author a contract and the author rejects it out of hand. Maybe they instead go in search of an editor who can guarantee publication or a PhD or who will promise to catch 100 percent of the errors. Maybe the author doesn't plan to pay you. Maybe the author was shocked that you want them to have responsibilities as well as rights. Maybe the contract prevented a professional dumpster fire.

Well, as a salesman friend says, "Sometimes the best deals are the deals you don't make."

5

THE ANATOMY OF A CONTRACT

1. The parties

The first thing you need to agree on is who the parties are. The person who has retained you may or may not be the author of the book you are agreeing to edit, for example.

2. Relationship of Parties

This clause reminds both of you that the client is not your boss. This means that you keep your own hours, you maintain your own equipment, and you don't punch a clock.

Your client wants that clause in there as much as you do. If your client treats you like an employee and you act like an employee, then your client might owe you things like sick leave or vacation time regardless of this contractual term. And he might have to make certain payroll deductions. There are tax consequences for both of you.

This clause establishes expectations and reminds both of you to stay in your lane. Obviously, you have spoken to your accountant about this.

And maybe to your therapist, too. You can include fuzzy language about professional conduct and mutual respect to place limits on client behavior. You do not want to work for someone who is manipulative or abusive or who wants to micromanage your work. How much of this to say explicitly is up to you, because you can solve all such problems retrospectively with a no-fault termination clause.

In my case, because I'm a lawyer, I have the following disclaimer in my contracts: "Editor does not have an attorney–client relationship with Client. Editor's work on the manuscript does not constitute legal advice." Why? Because the rules say that if I am going to establish an attorney–client relationship with someone, there has to be a written fee agreement. That's a separate contract that discusses scope of representation and the like. I'm not currently on active status with either Arizona or Virginia, and so I couldn't represent someone even if I wanted to. And even if I went back on active status, which would involve my taking some continuing legal education courses and paying the bar some money and buying malpractice insurance, I can't advise a client about events taking place outside Arizona or Virginia.

—KC

---

3. Furnished materials

Identify the material you are going to work on.

- This may be as specific as a particular filename with a particular date and time and an exact file size or word count.
- It may be a descriptive overview of a project, including the client's goals or intended use of the deliverable you are agreeing to provide.
- It may be a broad outline of a long-term engagement.

Why is this important? Because it helps you to avoid version control problems. When the author sends you an email telling you that you have begun work on the wrong document and sends you a version of *The Pirouette of the Manatee* that is 98,873 words, you can point to the contract and the word count of 97,019. When the author sends you the third version of *the Pirouette of the Manatee* in PDF format and demands that you edit *this* version, and what difference does it make, because you haven't started yet? You can point to the portion of the contract that says that you have agreed to work in Word.

If the job includes images and all you say is that the client will provide nine images but the ones provided are unusable because they're low-resolution screen shots, you can point to the requirement for furnished images that specifies the minimum resolution.

No, I meant the *other* other file
You have been retained to do a heavy copyedit. As you edit, the client keeps sending you revised manuscripts. You struggle to keep up, combining, editing, and re-editing whatever they send you, and you send them a finished manuscript on time. In a rage, they demand their money back. You have edited the wrong file.

Version Control

You don't want any questions about what thing it is that you are working on.

If the version you have has come from a third party—for example, because they referred the client to you—you can't ever assume that the client knows what version you have or whether it's the correct one. Email it back to the client: *Is this the version you want me to work with?* If they send you a different one, make sure that your price quote still applies. If they actually want you to work on a different version, make sure you get paid fairly. Revise your quote if you have to, and negotiate a new contract accordingly. No need for bait and switch, even by accident.

If that task gets away from you for some reason and a client complains, point them to the part of the contract that identifies the exact material you are working with. At that point, you have done your due diligence. You are not a mind reader.

One... Two... Three... Many

You have been retained to do a heavy copyedit of a 120,000-word science fiction book. You charged x cents a word. After you edit it, it's 80,000 words of pure gold. They publish it, and it's even sold 250 copies and counting! But they claim that they owe you x cents a word for *the number of words it is now* and not for how many words long the manuscript was when you got it. Who's right?

Be specific about when you count what.

- If you are charging by the word for editing a manuscript, are you charging by the number of words in the initial draft or in the final deliverable? And what happens if the client rewrites a thousand-word passage in response to a comment from you?
- If the author sends you twenty family photos to scan and ends up selecting ten to use in the book, how do you calculate the charges?

About this. One of the first client disputes I ever heard of as a new editor involved a price-per-word dispute. This happened to another editor. Their client insisted that the fee be calculated based on the length of the edited manuscript, which was a lot shorter than the original, and not on the length of the original manuscript.

I don't remember how that editor resolved the problem, but I never forgot it. So what I decided to do when

I charge by the word is give the client a total project fee based on word count. So if I charge *x* cents per word for a manuscript that is 97,019 words, I don't quote *x* cents per word. I multiply *x* cents per word by the 97,019 words, and that becomes the total project fee. They sign a contract that requires them to pay that total project fee, not *x* cents per word. It eliminates the confusion.

—KC

4. The Offer

Set out what you are proposing to do. Here is where you list, in as much detail as the client can absorb (or maybe a little more) what your offer consists of. If you list specific tasks by name, define them unambiguously. Say what is included and what is not included in each service you offer to perform.

Define the scope of the project, in other words, so it is clear to anyone reading the document what is included and what is not included.

Suppose, for example, you are proposing to edit a dissertation. You may feel the manuscript needs a *structural edit* as well as *heavy copyediting*. You know what you mean by those terms, but do you use them the same way another editor might? Will the client know what you mean? The answer to both of those questions is no.

And how does an author know that doing a structural and a line edit doesn't necessarily include editing for grammar, mechanics, spelling, usage, and punctuation? And if the author gets back a dissertation you've edited and you haven't touched the twelve hundred references, shouldn't that be by agreement? And if you are supposed to format the references and the two of you haven't discussed it, how are you supposed to know?

It's not necessarily true, by the way, that the author is going to be happy if you have a heavier hand with their manuscript than they thought you both bargained for. Maybe they were happy with their manuscript on the whole and they just wanted you to check and correct grammar, spelling, usage, and punctuation, but you sent it back with a line edit. Maybe you recast sentences, moved paragraphs around, or even deleted whole sections. Maybe the manuscript needed the involvement you provided. But the author didn't want it and didn't think they'd bargained for it.

Clients and service providers have an infinite number of ways to be unpleasantly surprised by differences of opinion about scope of work. Being as specific as possible protects both of you. The client is entitled to know what they are paying you for and you are entitled to do only the work that you're paid to do—and no more or no less.

> **I didn't know you meant I had to write it myself**
> You edit the manuscript, and they demand their money back. You only edited spelling, grammar, mechanics, usage, and punctuation, and they expected a partial rewrite, original research, and a chapter 1. That's because you told them that they really needed an introductory chapter that described the origins of the problem to start with. They assumed that your fee meant that you'd write it for them.

5. Schedule

For project-based contracts, most clients provide a deadline. This may be a deadline in the traditional sense of the word: it has to be done by a given date or the opportunity is missed. Or it may be a deadline in the more modern sense of the word: The client would like it by then, but no one will die if it's a few days late.

In either case, it is helpful to include a schedule in the contract. It should identify (typically in tabular form) the milestones, who is responsible for them, and when they are due. Obviously, you can only take responsibility for your own milestones. But when the client misses one, you can point to the clause that says any delay on the client's part propagates through the remainder of the schedule. Then you issue an amended schedule.

For large, complex projects with big teams, the project manager should be using dedicated scheduling software, and the contract can just incorporate the schedule by reference.

6. Conditions

Once burned, twice shy.

You have identified the parties and their relationship to one another. You have described the nature of the project and the services you are offering to perform. Do you need to do anything more before seeking the client's acceptance of your offer, other than saying what all this work is going to cost?

Yes. If you have spent an idle hour perusing any discussion forum where creative professionals gather, you have encountered horror stories of assumptions proven wrong, of gross misunderstandings, of ignorance triumphant over sense.

What you call this section of the contract can affect how the client perceives it. Remembering that your contract is part of your sales effort, you might want to give it a neutral title or no title at all. Consider using bullets rather than paragraph numbers, which are more legalistic-looking.

Some of the conditions you may want to include in your contract are discussed below. The sample contracts in the appendix list others that may be useful.

Standards
What standards apply to the job? Some ideas to consider:

- For an editing job, what dictionary and style guide will be used? What specialized dictionaries and guides apply? Does the client have a house style that must be followed?

- Will errors be preserved in material quoted from published sources, or will minor corrections for spelling and punctuation be made silently? Will speech errors be preserved in transcribed material or smoothed out to preserve the speaker's intent?
- What variety of English is involved? What register is desired? Is there a specific measure of readability that must be achieved, such as the controversial Flesch-Kincaid grade level score, or is the editor permitted to use their own judgment about such things?
- Does the editing brief include markup for composition?
- Does it include proofreading?
- How will consistency, accuracy, and completeness be measured and what level is sufficient?
- For a page layout job, how many lines in succession can end in a hyphen? Can a word be broken on the last line of a verso page? A recto page? What constitutes a bad break? Are orphans acceptable? Are widows acceptable? What rules apply to consistency of page depth?

Expiration

How long is the offer valid for? You don't want to offer services today and have the client return the acceptance three years from now, expecting to honor today's prices and schedule. Depending on circumstances, you may decide that the offer is valid for three months or a month or a week or a day or fifteen minutes. What is expiring is the offer, not the contract. Once the contract takes effect, it remains in effect until the job is done or the termination clause has been invoked.

Confidentiality

You may decide to have a separate confidentiality agreement before you even send a proposal to the prospective client. Or you may be okay with simply stating that the proposal is confidential. What you are trying to avoid is a client forwarding your proposal to a competitor of yours who can look it over and come back with a bid a few dollars less than yours.

Rights
Does the client have the right to publish the material, or does it belong to someone else? Plagiarism is not always intentional, because many clients don't have a clue. How often have you heard a tenured faculty member assert that anything published on the internet is in the public domain? The question applies to text as well as to images.

Liability
What happens if there's plagiarism and you don't catch it? What happens if someone believes the content defames them or violates their right to privacy or infringes on their copyright?

Any resemblance to persons living or dead
The manuscript is a literary novel about a grocery store clerk and his love of a woman who goes through his checkout line every week. Your edits turn it from a good novel to a great one. Then a lawyer out of left field sends you a demand letter for more money than you will ever make in your life. It seems that the author is a woman, and a grocery store clerk has hired the lawyer because the grocery store clerk is a married man who claims that the grocery store clerk depicted in the novel is unmistakably him. As a result, his husband now thinks he was having an affair and has left him. The grocery store clerk is suing the author, and you, for portraying him in a false light—which is a tort.

You may want to cover this potential issue ahead of time with an attorney. There are a couple of things going on here. You can edit, you can comment, you can query, you can delete. You still have no control over what goes into the finished manuscript. And, as in the grocery clerk scenario, there can be a stealth legal issue with a manuscript. You have no way of knowing that there's a problem until you find out that it's a problem. And your role here is one of editor, not media lawyer.

Some stuff in a manuscript that could be defamatory might not be. If you are concerned about that, flag it with a comment like "Consider discussing this passage with a defamation lawyer." With content that really makes your hair stand on end, delete it. In this way, you have communicated as strongly as possible that you object to the presence of the relevant text in the manuscript. If they want it in their manuscript so badly, they can bloody well put it back themselves.

Is all of this a violation of the principal that editors have no right to impose their preferences on a manuscript? Well, sort of. But you don't want to have the daylights sued out of you because a client has written that, based on the way their aunt's new husband dresses, he is obviously a pedophile. Does that count as a preference?

How do you know what language in your manuscript needs to be treated that way? Like porn, you'll know it when you see it. Or maybe you won't, which is why this clause. After all, who could have seen the grocery store clerk coming?

You want the client to indemnify you if someone sues you for failing to prevent the problem, even if you tried and the client overruled you. Don't discount the possibility that the client will sue you, because the client's liability carrier may do that in the client's name, completely out of the client's control.

This brings up another problem. If you have assets (you own your home, for example) and the client is an impecunious grad student with no insurance, then it really doesn't matter if the client agrees to indemnify you, because they have nothing to indemnify you with. If the client objects to your running a credit check on them, or if they acknowledge they're poor as a church mouse, then consider having the contract giving you final say on material you want to delete.

5 • The Anatomy of a Contract • 27

Schedule Contingency
You need to ensure that the client will respond to you in a timely manner when you have an urgent question.

> You are a third of the way into a manuscript when you discover that a large chunk of it is missing or has been digested by Word into a pile of indecipherable gobbledygook. You send an email to the client. The client checks email once every three weeks regular as clockwork, and that was yesterday. But you still have a deadline.

The client has an obligation to participate in the process as needed, and failing to do so may delay final delivery. You have to account for this in the contract, particularly if delay costs you money or causes you to lose other business.

Out-of-Scope Work
Things happen. Sometimes you get into the middle of a project and suggest the client add new material. That bumps up the scale of the project. Or the client decides to rewrite chapter 3 after you've finished the first pass on it. Whatever. How will such out-of-scope work be handled? How will you calculate extra charges? Say it now to avoid arguments later.

> **The guy across the street isn't the only scope creep**
> You have agreed to edit a textbook and complete the edits in sixty days. You get a frantic email from the project manager and they have moved up the deadline by three weeks. You get another frantic email. Not only are you to format the references, you are to complete them. This means research. There are about three thousand references in this entire textbook, and, upon first glance, about

a third of them are incomplete. And then you get a call. They need you to rework the tables in chapter 3. Then you get a call directly from one of the authors. They need to spend an hour on the phone with you next week because you will need to make changes and it's easier to do it over the phone.

Expenses
How will you be compensated for expenses you incur on the client's behalf? Do you need the client's credit card information? If the client asks you to travel for a meeting—or if you have to go downtown to the main library to examine a reference document that's not available online—how will you be compensated for the travel time?

Credits, acknowledgments, complimentary copies, and sales reports
Some manuscripts are guaranteed problems. Either the author isn't going to accept changes, or you think they will make additions after you have finished, and so you risk having a reviewer say "Where was the editor?!" when the answer is "being ignored." Alternatively, you may find offensive content that the author declines to change.

Will you be credited publicly on the client's website or in the finished product? Do you have the right to review any written acknowledgment, correct factual errors (like your name being misspelled), or refuse to be mentioned (because you gave the client a clean file and the client introduced a dozen errors afterward)? Will you be given a complimentary copy—or two or five or ... — of the finished product? Will the client provide reports on the commercial success of the project (if that's something you want to know about)?

Risks
You are not Procter & Gamble. You cannot guarantee "satisfaction or your money back." You cannot guarantee that the finished project will accomplish what the client hopes it will accomplish.

You cannot guarantee perfect work, either.

By the time the client decided to work with you, they had almost certainly considered your training and experience, work samples, perhaps a phone conversation with them about their work, and maybe references or reputation. So the client presumably understands that you are going to act professionally and do the best job you can within the time and budget allotted for it. That's really all you can promise. Most professionals agree that correcting 95 percent of errors is the industry standard.

What happens if you really screw up and the client has good reason to be unhappy with your work? Instead of acknowledging that you're too sick to work and you can't make the deadline, for example, you power through and deliver work that is below your standards.

What can you say in the contract about that situation?

Finally, identify the risks that are beyond your control. You and your client should acknowledge that risks exist despite everyone's best efforts to mitigate them. Spell out what they are:

- The best laid plans of mice and men gang aft agley. The project may be late for reasons outside your control. But in particular, if the client doesn't live up to their obligations, you're not going to deliver on time. If you estimate 50 hours for a project and the client supplies you with their draft 30 hours before the deadline, you can't perform—not unless they have invented a time machine.

AU: Failure to plan on your part . . .
You agree to edit a book-length dissertation with a very tight deadline. If it isn't turned in on time, the author won't be awarded a PhD and won't even graduate on time. You know that it will take weeks to edit. You have budgeted that time into your calendar, and you have other manuscripts that are due later. But the author doesn't send you the manuscript, so you turn your attention to other projects.

Finally, the frantic author sends you the manuscript. If you don't start now, you won't meet their deadline, but if you do start now, you'll be late on other projects.

- The final cost may be higher than the initial estimate, particularly if the client doesn't furnish materials in the specified condition on the specified schedule or if the scope changes.
- To err is human. You are not guaranteeing perfection. But if the furnished materials are rife with errors, you're gonna need a bigger boat, er, budget to get to an acceptable level.
- The hardest thing to predict is the future: you cannot guarantee that the project will be a financial success.

Deliverables

What are you going to deliver to your client as output? What are you not going to deliver? This question goes to your own business practices as well as the client's requirements—and often the client's technical abilities.

Will your obligation be fulfilled with delivery of a Word file with changes tracked, for the client to take it from there? Or will you be responsible for cleaning up a reviewed file and delivering it with all changes accepted? What if there are unresolved queries because the client didn't bother to answer them?

Do you retain ownership of your work product, or does everything belong to the client? For example, if you have done work in Photoshop or InDesign, does the client get your Photoshop and InDesign files or only finished image files and PDFs?

Delivery

How and when do you deliver the files, and how and when do you get paid?

Does the client expect you to print the final manuscript and send it overnight via FedEx Or fax it to them!), or have you agreed to send the file as an email attachment? If it's too big for email, can the client access it via Dropbox? If not, do you have to ship a USB stick?

If the project deadline is critical, you and your client need to agree on times and time zones. If your client lives in a time zone that's eight hours ahead of yours and they are waiting for you to complete your job at 5:00 p.m. their time, and that's their drop-dead deadline, but you think it's due at 5:00 p.m. your time . . . well, this is why we can't have nice things.

Take Daylight Saving Time (DST) into account too. On the date the project is delivered, one of you may be on DST and the other may not. Some US states don't observe it, and different countries change to or from DST on different dates, depending on their latitude or their political choices. Go to www.timeanddate.com/time/dst/ and click the link that reads "DST changes: Dates and local times." The page that loads provides information for the current year.

I'm a freelance editor because my kid has special needs and there may be appointments—foreseen or not. Or he may have had a remarkable day at school and need to process it with me. When Arizona's teachers were on strike, my kid was out of school. Since he supported their cause, he insisted on attending their rally at the state capital. That took all morning. I didn't get back to my desk until after 3:00 p.m.

If I spend my morning at an IEP meeting or an appointment or emergency visit to one of his providers I don't want to stare at the clock and fear the end of the business day while my stomach slowly begins to digest itself. And while it is true that I have gotten some really good work done in doctor's office waiting rooms, I'd really prefer not to need to. So I give myself the option of having complete freedom to deal with kid emergencies and appointments during the business day and work in the afternoon and evening. My deadline is 11:59 p.m. You may prefer to roll up your streets by five. Either way, make sure that you and your client metaphorically synchronize your watches.

—KC

We do business with clients all over the world, so it's important to stipulate what currency you are working with.

I was shocked when I did a currency conversion and realized that a client's budget was actually $27.00. If I had just included their number and assumed that it was in US dollars, things could have gone very badly very quickly. As it was, I had to turn down the work. This was a $2,000 project, not a $20 one!

—KC

---

7. Consideration

You have carefully laid out the offer in exquisite detail. You have added language to prevent every foreseeable disaster. Now it is time to let the client know what your professional services are worth.

If you quote a lump sum for the whole project and both parties discover that out-of-scope work is essential, there are a couple of ways to handle this. The worst way is to eat the cost.

KC prefers to negotiate an amendment to the contract or a separate service agreement. During a short sample edit, she learned that one client felt most comfortable with a thirty-minute phone call, so worked that preference into the service agreement for the whole project by including an hourly phone-call surcharge.

Similarly, if the client is late on their review step and they want to pay you a rush charge to catch up, if the libel lawyer cuts 20,000 words from the manuscript before it gets to you—you need to negotiate an amendment to the contract.

DM prefers to list prices for units of work. So much a word or so much a page. So much per reference or per image. Such-and-such a percentage surcharge for rush work. So much an hour for out-of-scope work. And so on. These are the line items you will put on your invoice, and they will match the contract. If the contract says $0.04 a word, then the invoice will say 62,583 words @ $0.04, with an extension (quantity times price) of $ 2,503.32. This is straightforward.

The down side is that clients want to know what the whole project will cost. So you need to prepare a separate document that is an estimate of all charges. Be sure to make clear that the estimate is *not* a quote. The list of prices in the proposal is the quote, and invoices will be based on the quote, not on the estimate.

8. Termination

The relationship between you and your client can become irretrievably broken. Perhaps the client calls constantly or sends abusive messages. Perhaps the manuscript is plagiarized. Perhaps the client has difficulty with boundaries. Or, conversely, sometimes a client is hit with an unexpected expense or they lose a job, or you become seriously ill or injured. It's important to have some kind of mechanism in place to allow you and your client to part company in a fair and orderly way and preferably without hard feelings.

If the client walks away from a nonrefundable deposit, that's the client's loss. If you terminate the agreement, you deserve to keep the portion of the deposit you've earned. You should probably refund any unearned portion. If the client behaves badly, you might be tempted to say that you're terminating the agreement *for cause* and that you deserve to keep the full deposit.

KC has a termination fee. If the client walks away from the project, she keeps the nonrefundable deposit. She collects installment payments throughout the project, and at each step, if a client walks, she keeps an incremental portion of the fees. She also has a line in her contract that says she does not return unfinished manuscripts. When a client books an editor for a set period, the editor naturally doesn't schedule other work for the same time. If a project evaporates, the editor doesn't earn money if they can't fill the empty slot. If she were to have to terminate a project, she would be paid for the work she has done.

DM feels that keeping the deposit of a client who behaves badly would invite trouble you don't need. A litigious client can ruin your whole day.

9. Warranties

Your contract lists the standards the work will be measured against. It lists the risks that are beyond your control. But what if the work falls short of the standards, and it really is your fault? The client deserves some protection against paying for unsatisfactory work, if the work is measured against an objective standard.

For time-critical projects that you deliver late, you can negotiate a penalty clause with the client. It might say that for each day the project is late due to your fault, you will refund a certain amount of money. For projects where the number of residual errors is the critical factor, you might build in a quality control inspection by a third party and accept responsibility for making additional corrections at no charge to bring the work up to the agreed standard.

10. Legal Boilerplate

Lawyers deal in worst-case scenarios, and they have learned that to protect their clients from bad outcomes, they have to include certain standard clauses in contracts. Litigating a contract in court is a bad outcome whether you win or lose the case, so anything you can include in the contract to prevent going to court is a good thing.

Clients who have any experience with contracts (even their apartment leases) will not be surprised to see these clauses.

KC had a client who balked at certain elements of the service agreement because he felt that it presumed that he would be dishonest. She explained to him, truthfully, that her then-current apartment lease said she couldn't run a meth lab out of the apartment. The apartment complex was in a very nice, low-crime area. She pointed out that that addendum to the lease was undoubtedly put there because it came up somewhere else with someone else and they wanted to be able to evict drug dealers from the complex. The clause even noted that a conviction was not required. KC pointed out to the author that she was certain that the apartment management company did not suspect her of running a meth lab, or of planning to run a meth lab, and that it was not personal, but it was a boilerplate contract because they couldn't tell in advance who planned to start one. The author found the analogy apt, and also funny, and signed KC's service agreement; and the business relationship was a fruitful one.

Severability

If a court rules that one part of this whole contract is not valid for some reason, the whole contract is invalid, unless you include a severability clause.

Applicable Laws and Jurisdiction

You may have clients from all over the world. If a client in another country—or even a neighboring state—doesn't pay you, you don't want to have to travel there. But venue is a thing, and choice of law is a thing, too, and you don't want to have to litigate that. You not only want to be able to drive to the courthouse up the street, but you also want the lawyer you hire to know what the law is where you are.

Or Not

If you are dealing with serious money—more than, say, $50,000—you want a contract that your attorney is confident will stand up in a court of law. That's just common sense.

But most of us are dealing, most of the time, with projects on a smaller scale. And you have to ask yourself whether it would ever be sensible to pay a lawyer to settle a dispute. If you are smart in the way you construct your contract, you should be able to stay out of court, even small claims court, forever.

If your client agrees that the purpose of the contract is to align expectations and that you both want to stay out of court, you can include language that says the amount of money at stake is insufficient to justify paying lawyers and that the sole remedy in any dispute is to invoke the termination clause.

You can also agree that mediation or arbitration is the only remedy. But you still want your contract to specify that the location of that event is convenient to you.

11. Changes

You need a mechanism for amending the contract. You can just say it can be amended by written agreement and that an exchange of email messages acknowledging the change will suffice. Or, if that makes you uncomfortable, you can require a signed written addendum.

12. Payment Terms

Craft the payment terms to match the situation.

- On the first project with an individual client, you are going to want a nonrefundable deposit large enough to compensate you for dealing with someone who disappears after they send you

the manuscript and large enough to discourage them from disappearing. And then you want to continue to work behind the payments. That is, you always want the money in hand before you do the work. You want the last payment in hand before you deliver the final product. Be as explicit as you can in laying out a schedule of progress payments. They can be tied to milestones or to dates.
- For clients you've learned to trust, you can bill as you go along. And for corporate clients, you're going to be stuck billing according to their schedule.

Late Fees
For everyone, the terms include language about late payment. If you only do work after you get the money, then the language has to point to the effect on the planned project schedule. Otherwise, though, you need to write terms that comply with applicable law. If you are in the United States and you are adding a finance charge, the language and the math have to follow the Truth in Lending Act of 1968: you can apply simple interest but not compound interest; you have to state both the monthly percentage and the annual percentage rate (APR). The APR also has to comply with your state's usury law.

Another approach is to forgo the finance charge and instead impose a service charge, such as a flat $25.00 late payment fee that you add every month when you send out a new statement.

But you can't add a finance charge or a rebilling fee or a late payment fee on an invoice unless you've already included it in the contract.

Release of Copyright
You can claim a copyright interest in material you've worked on that you will release upon payment. This is additional leverage if for some reason you aren't paid in advance.

13. Acceptance

The client's acceptance of the proposal, with whatever modifications the two of you have agreed to, is what indicates that a meeting of the minds has occurred. How does the client signify acceptance?

- You can provide a space for the client to initial each page of the agreement (typically in the lower right corner).
- Any last-minute changes handwritten in the agreement should be initialed in ink by each of you.
- At the end of the contract, include spaces for you and the client to sign and date the document. If the client is a company, then the individual signing for the company should say what their role or title is (this goes for you, too, if you are representing a business).

The old-fashioned way is to print two copies and do all the above initialing and signing in ink. You are welcome to use a more modern procedure. But it must be unambiguous that the signature, whether digital or analog, applies to the entire document.

Adobe Acrobat has a signature function that allows you to basically sign the screen and then preserves that signature for use as a stamp. This prevents you from having to print the contract, scan it, and email it.

6

REMEDIES

What if the worst happens? What if you don't take your fees in advance? Or what if they pay you by PayPal and then demand a refund? PayPal will give it to them and then make you fight for your money back.

Let's assume the following:

- Your client owes you the money
- You have sent them an invoice
- Your client is actually late paying
- Your client has either explicitly stated a refusal to pay or declined to pay despite repeated requests
- You have asked directly, you have sent an invoice, and you have given them time to respond

And now what? Do you stampede to the courthouse? Not necessarily. If it's an academic book, you can certainly show the publisher that clause in your contract that says that you retain copyright interest in the edited manuscript until paid in full. Do they want to mess around with a copyright infringement suit? You can also raise the issue of nonpayment with a student's dissertation supervisor. The conduct of a student can reflect badly on a school, and many schools have honor codes.

You can send a demand letter, telling them you will send the matter to collections.

You can also sue them.

Some people think that it's too expensive to sue for the fee because it will cost more than the lawsuit is worth. But talk to a lawyer. Most government entities that confer law licenses (like the state bar) have a referral service, where you can get the names of lawyers in your subject area. You can also get names by word of mouth.

Most lawyers will agree to a one-hour consultation. Be up front that that is what you are asking for. Do it as soon as you see a problem. It's never too soon to talk to a lawyer. Depending on the lawyer, that can run you anywhere from $300 to $500. Maybe the client doesn't owe you that much. Maybe you think that it will cost you more to sue than it would to let the money go. Maybe you're afraid that the client will be angry with you if you do that.

About the client being angry at you? Do yourself a favor for a second: Look around you. What do you see? Your refrigerator? Is there anything in it? If you flip on a light switch, can you see better? Do you have a roof over your head? You're not at home, you say? Were you wearing shoes when you left? Think about not having any of those things.

Now think about the client being angry at you because they say they don't want to pay you what they owe you.

So the next question is, is it worth it? There are a lot of issues to consider. First, there's that meeting with the lawyer to have. And you want to know if you can file in small claims court. (Because you'd be surprised how much money you can sue for in small claims court. In some places, that's as much as $10,000.00.) Do you have to have a lawyer in order to file? Can you afford to walk away from the money? Are you concerned about this client doing this to other editors?

If you plan to sue them, you might have to send them a demand letter telling them that you're about to file the lawsuit. You might want to send them that demand letter because people don't want to be sued, and they don't want an unsatisfied judgment affecting their credit.

Any time that you sue an individual or an entity, the other party has to have notice of the lawsuit and an opportunity to be heard. If they don't have that notice, you can't go forward with the lawsuit. There are technicalities for how to serve the other party, particularly if they live overseas or out of state. On the other hand, one of the ways to serve the lawsuit might (*might*) be by publication, which is not expensive. A lawyer can advise you on how to properly serve someone in a lawsuit. Some courts even have a website with a self-service section with forms, and that website may have a list of ways to serve someone that is appropriate for your jurisdiction.

If they are properly served, and they don't appear, you may be able to win a default judgment. If they do show, and you can show the court the signed contract, it improves your position. If you win a judgment, you may be able to ask for costs—such as the costs of service and attorneys' fees—depending on local law. That doesn't mean that you will be able to collect on the judgment. You may just end up with a document suitable for framing.

On the other hand, the mere filing of the lawsuit might encourage them to pay. Because if they don't pay, and they have the unsatisfied judgment, it might affect their ability to borrow money. It may also have other effects on them, such as their ability to obtain a security clearance. It might affect the interest rates on their credit cards.

Again, you may want to consult with a lawyer about the ins and outs of local practice, even if you don't bring the lawyer to court with you. You might also discuss any vulnerabilities to your position, or any allegations they might make. You might want to discuss how local courts respond to lawsuits like this.

You may decide that the amount of money isn't worth the hassle, and it might not be. Only you can decide that.

One thing. If you do have vulnerabilities in your case, you may bring on a countersuit, and you will have to defend it. The more specific your contract, the better your position. A specific contract even helps you know whether problems with your own performance merit your deciding to walk away from the entire situation happy that it's behind you. At that point, perhaps chalk it up to a learning experience and move on.

I keep telling you that you might want an hour with an attorney. I'm not just saying that. If there are any meaningful stakes involved in a situation, it's better to consult with an attorney as soon as you think there might be a problem. What you don't want is for a demand letter from a client to cross your desk and wait until you are served and a hearing is imminent to get the name of an attorney and try to get in to see them. It won't go well. In fact, if a client behaves in a way that makes you even think they might sue, then the moment that thought occurs to you is the moment to call a lawyer. They might help you avoid problems ahead of time, even—or perhaps especially—if you messed up.

–KC

7

DISSERTATIONS

You agree to edit a dissertation. You think that you're doing a copyedit. You correct spelling, grammar, mechanics, and usage. You tighten up sentences and shorten paragraphs. The writing is a little turgid, and so you streamline it. You turn it in on time. The author is furious. They expected you to improve the structure of the manuscript, do some original research, coach them on content, and help them with their argument. They'd really appreciate it if you could write their abstract for them, too. They have to defend the dissertation in three weeks, and there is no way they can finish on time.

There are two problems with this situation. First, there is no meeting of the minds, since there is no explicit document setting out the services that you will provide, and second, some of these services are unethical for you to perform for a dissertation author. Part of the reason that PhD candidates write dissertations is to show that they know how to do all of the things you have to know how to do to call yourself a researcher. That means that the content, the organization, the argument, the proof, the structure, all have to be the work of the student. You can't ethically do that work for them and it's highly unlikely that their school is going to permit them to have that kind of work done.

Maybe the school is fine with it. Maybe the dissertation supervisor is AWOL for some reason. Maybe the dissertation supervisor got severely ill. Maybe the dissertation supervisor passed away. Maybe the dissertation supervisor knows that the student needs extra help and believes that you can provide it. Maybe it's early enough in the

43

process and the student would benefit from your instruction. After all, we editors teach our clients how to write better by showing them, and often by explaining the reason for a change. Perhaps you can provide a high level of editing. Your student still needs the explicit permission of the department or they could get expelled. Is that what you want?

It might be tempting to suggest that no one would ever know, or if you don't do it someone else would, or it's the student's job to take care of that and not yours. Maybe you have the best of intentions. Maybe the student really is being neglected by their dissertation supervisor. But how are you going to feel if your client gets expelled?

Even work that might be ethically fine might not be if your student doesn't clear it with their supervisor. KC does this kind of work:

- format to requirements of APA [for example] and university template
- copyedit for grammar, spelling, mechanics, and usage
- tighten up sentences
- eliminate wordiness
- adjust paragraph length
- ensure that references are in the correct format
- flag items in the reference list that are not cited in the manuscript
- flag citations that are not in the reference list
- flag incomplete references
- ensure that lists and items in charts and tables are parallel in construction
- ensure that tables and text match
- ensure that acronyms are defined before use, aren't defined twice, and aren't used at all if the term isn't used more than once
- format chapter heads and page numbers
- make a table of contents

This list is in KC's version of the Dissertation Supervisor Agreement Form that Editors Canada has on its website. Her version of the form is in the back of this book. She can perform fewer services if a student wants. She's formatted references and nothing else. But for ethical reasons, she will not write someone's dissertation abstract or help them with their argument.

Her agreement form goes to the student to be signed by their dissertation supervisors. This protects the student from allegations of academic dishonesty. It prevents her from being complicit in someone else's academic dishonesty. And everyone goes away happy.

You may have other services that you provide. Some editors are much more comprehensive in what the relevant contract doesn't provide.

OTHER PEOPLE'S CONTRACTS

Nondisclosures

As you send your client a service agreement, they may be sending you a nondisclosure agreement (NDA) and a noncompetition agreement. Should you sign these?

It depends. If your client is an individual who has written their first novel, the client is of the opinion that their story is worth a million dollars and anyone with the opportunity to steal it will do so, depriving them of fame and fortune. It is important to quash this delusion as soon as possible. No matter what the NDA says, you should refuse on principle to sign it, and you should counsel the author that no editor, agent, or publisher will work with an author who insists on an NDA.

But if your client is a corporation engaging you to put the finishing touches on the marketing materials for a product they haven't announced, or if you are editing documents for a law firm, or if you are working on a financial disclosure document, then it's perfectly reasonable for them to expect you to sign an NDA. Movie scripts, too, are a type of manuscript for which an NDA is often requested. So are documents protected by HIPAA.

Sensible NDAs provide reasonable protections for both parties. There should be a clause excluding any information you could have obtained from published sources. (Some US government agencies are famous for clipping articles from newspapers for their files and stamping them Top Secret.) You should be exempt from responsibility for disclosures that you have nothing to do with. The scope of the NDA should be limited to proprietary information the client discloses to you so that you can do the job they are engaging you to do. And the NDA should expire when the information is eventually made public.

The nondisclosure agreement nominally protects the author's intellectual property. Depending on how these agreements are worded, though, they can be a nightmare for a scrupulous editor. For instance, they may be so broadly worded that you couldn't ever even get your computer fixed, and you have to pay damages if the author thinks there has been an inappropriate disclosure even if you had nothing to do with the disclosure. The remedy could be unconscionable. Or they may prohibit you from disclosing material that you might otherwise be obligated to disclose by law (or the nondisclosure of which might open you up to civil liability). For instance, what if the manuscript turns out to contain the author's admission that they have committed child sexual assault? What if it contains a threat to a third party, or doxxes someone?

Generally, courts have been skeptical of NDAs, especially those drawn for nefarious purposes. But you don't want to have to go to court to defend yourself. So you're better off negotiating a reasonable agreement or walking away if you can't.

Because an NDA can have far-reaching consequences, it is best to contact an attorney if you have any concerns about a particular NDA that is presented to you.

Non-competes

If you get clients through an agency, that agency doesn't want you waltzing away with their clients and cutting them out of the picture. The agency will ask you to sign a non-compete agreement. What it boils down to is that you can't work for the same client independently that you worked for through the agency. Nor do they want you to solicit other clients of theirs that you might become aware of.

This can create some sticky situations. What happens if you stop working for the agency, and one of their clients approaches you directly? What happens if the agency is in trouble financially and stops paying its editors? What happens if the author severs its agreement with the agency because they had a bad experience but they liked your work? Are those and similar situations contemplated in the way the agreement is worded?

Beyond those reasonable questions, which can be difficult to negotiate, there are more dangerous shoals. Some non-compete clauses would bar you from ever working on another document in the same field. Someone hires you because you have expertise in a particular subject and then wants to tell you can never edit another book about that subject? Um, no.

NDAs can be problematic. Non-competes can be disastrous. Courts have been reluctant to enforce them, because they tend to have the effect of limiting someone's ability to earn a living. But you don't want to go to court. If you can't persuade the prospective client to drop the requirement altogether, either run it by a lawyer or walk away.

"Contractor" contracts

You are engaged to edit a manuscript for a faculty member at a state university. State law requires that you sign a contract. The department secretary contacts the comptroller's office and asks for a contract to send to you. Oh, here's the form right here. Says "Contractor" on top. This must be the one.

The problem, as many editors have discovered, is that when a state university comptroller hears the word *contractor*, they immediately think of a construction contractor coming on campus to remodel an existing building or construct some new facility. They are not thinking about you.

As a result, the boilerplate contract presented to you requires that you post a bond; that you carry a million dollars' worth of liability insurance, a separate policy to cover any injury caused by a motor vehicle (you're never going to set foot on campus, which may be several time zones away from you); and all sorts of other protections and indemnifications that construction contractors deal with routinely but that have nothing whatsoever to do with what you're being engaged to perform.

This is all nonsense, of course. But you have to work your way up the chain to someone in a position of authority who can sign off on crossing out the irrelevant clauses or who knows where to find a different contract form to substitute for the construction contract. This generally goes more smoothly at private institutions, because they do not have state auditors breathing down their necks. But with patience, the help of the department chair, and lots of deep cleansing breaths, you should eventually prevail.

The mechanics is simple. Draw a line through the offending language, and write your initials near the change. If the other party initials the change, you have a meeting of the minds. If they don't, you don't have a contract.

Client-supplied editing contracts

Publishers often have their own contracts. If you want the work, you probably have to accept their terms. However, publishers come in all shapes and sizes and levels of legal sophistication, and you should never sign a contract you haven't read and don't understand.

Publishing lawyers know all about publishing law, but they may be pressed into service to craft an editing contract, where it's also important to understand something about employment law. The principal risk (in the United States, at least) is that a badly drawn contract can create a set of conditions where the Internal Revenue Service will determine, when they audit the publisher several years hence, that you were not, in fact, an independent contractor but were instead an employee.

On the one hand, the liability in that case falls mostly on the publisher. You might even get a nice-sized windfall. But there could also be consequences for you that you didn't plan for. The way to avoid this situation is to watch out for this issue when you're reading the contract before signing it. If the publisher is both paying you by the hour and telling you what hours they expect you to work, for example, they may be pushing up against the boundary of how tightly they can control an independent contractor.

9

CONCLUSION

This little booklet contains basic business advice for editors who blanch when they hear the word *contract*. It isn't a legal textbook, and it doesn't take the place of consultation with a lawyer. It's meant to make you more comfortable thinking and talking about contracts and using them as a business tool to help you grow your editing business. It's meant, too, to make you more comfortable to think of yourself as owning and running a business in the first place.

APPENDIX: SAMPLE CONTRACTS

How you construct the contract should reflect the type of relationship you want to have with your clients. We present here our two very different templates, both of which include all of the main points discussed in the preceding chapters.

SAMPLE #1: KARIN'S TEMPLATE

1. The parties

This service agreement is between Karin Cather Editorial Services LLC d/b/a Karin Cather ("Editor") and John Ocelot ("Client") and concerns the following manuscript:

> **Author(s):** John Ocelot

2. The manuscript

> **Working title:** *The Pirouette of the Manatee* ("the manuscript")
>
> **Length and description of the manuscript:** A Word document of approximately 97,019 words.

3. Relationship of Parties

Editor is a freelance service provider and is not an employee of John Ocelot.

> **Note**
> What follows is a list of tasks that the client and you can choose from, sort of like a build-your-own six-pack of artisanal beer. Only with a lot less drinking.

This is not an exhaustive list, but it's illustrative of the amount of detail KC goes into in her contracts.

There are many ways for authors and editors to be unpleasantly surprised by differences of opinion about scope of work. Being as specific as possible protects both of you.

---

4. Editorial Tasks

Editor shall:
- Where necessary for narrative clarity and quality, move chapters, sections, or paragraphs from one place to another.
- Where necessary to ensure that the paragraph has a clear and coherent focus, reorder sentences within paragraphs.
- Delete material that is redundant or detracts from the narrative, or flag such material that, in editor's judgment, should be deleted.
- Determine the language and reading level appropriate for the intended audience and medium, and edit to establish or maintain that language and level.
- Establish or maintain a consistent tone, style, and authorial voice or level of formality appropriate for the intended audience and medium.
- Flag sentences or paragraphs that require further development by author for effective narrative quality and flow.
- Adjust the length and structure of paragraphs to ensure variety or consistency, as appropriate to the audience and medium.
- Ensure that transitions between sentences and between paragraphs are smooth and support the coherent development of the text as a whole.
- Only where necessary, rewrite sentences, paragraphs, or passages to resolve ambiguities, ensure logical connections, and clarify the

author's meaning or intention, in harmony with the style of the material. Does not include research or writing original material.
- Render jargon into plain language while leaving terms of art intact.
- Ensure correctness and consistency of spelling, mechanics, usage, and punctuation.
- Fact-check existing manuscript or do research to permit author to develop or expand existing manuscripts.
- Ensure that manuscript conforms to the appropriate style manual and dictionary.
- In fiction, recommend changes in pacing and plot.
- In fiction, recommend changes in dialogue to ensure that diction, tone, and vocabulary are consistent with character's age, occupation, life experiences, and educational background.
- Provide original writing to expand existing manuscript or ghostwrite document as a whole [this will require payment of an hourly rate].
- In fiction, identify characters who should get more or less time on the stage or whether they should be cut from the manuscript.
- In nonfiction, recommend that certain ideas be developed further or cut from the manuscript for use in a second publication.
- Eliminate wordiness.
- Make sure that text boxes and tables are clear and coherent and that captions fairly describe them.
- Make sure that text boxes and tables add to the clarity and coherence of the manuscript.
- Ensure that headings, tables, and footnotes are clearly and sequentially numbered
- Where necessary, write original material [for purpose stated here]
- Where necessary, conduct original research [for purpose stated here]

Note: The editing tasks exclude proofreading.

First of all, why not proofreading? Because this is my contract and I am not a proofreader. Also, if I am adding text or rewriting things, someone else is going to have to edit for typos for the same reason that an author has hired you.

—KC

---

5. Version Control

Between the time Editor begins work pursuant to this service agreement and the time Editor returns edited manuscript to Client, Client shall not make any revisions to the manuscript. After Editor submits the final manuscript to Client, any further work on the manuscript shall be the subject of a separate service agreement.

6. Delivery

a) Client shall return the signed service agreement and the complete manuscript, and pay the first installment of $x,500.00 to Editor on or before January 1, 2019 at 11:59 p.m. Arizona time.
b) Client shall pay Editor a second installment of $x,500.00 on or before January 15, 2019 at 11:59 p.m. Arizona time.
c) Editor shall complete the editing tasks on or before January 30, 2019 at 11:59 p.m. Arizona time, and deliver edited manuscript to Client.

All work on the manuscript shall be performed electronically, on the Word document, and not on a hard copy. Delivery of the manuscript shall by effectuated by email. Editor's email address is Karin@catheredit.com. Client can be reached at JohntheOtter@verderiver.com.

7. Effect of Delays

If Client does not provide Editor with a copy of the manuscript, signed service agreement, dissertation supervisor agreement form, relevant university style guide (if any), and first installment by January 1, 2019, Editor shall not start work, and the deadlines may have to be revisited subject to Editor's availability. If Client does not pay second installment by January 15, 2019, Editor shall stop work and resumption of work will require a new agreement, contingent on availability.

Please note that signed service agreement means the entire service agreement with a signature, not merely the page with the signature on it.

Editor will not deliver unfinished manuscript to Client and will not deliver any manuscript unless paid in full.

8. Payment

The agreed-upon editorial fee of a first installment of $x,500.00; a second installment of $x,500.00; for a total amount of $x,000.00 shall be paid to the Editor via PayPal (Karin@catheredit.com).

Client shall pay the first installment on or before January 1, 2019 at 11:59 p.m. Arizona time, the second installment on or before January 15, 2019 at 11:59 p.m. Arizona time.

> You'll note that I insist on getting paid before the client gets their manuscript back. This is almost always nonnegotiable when I am dealing with an individual client.

9. Termination

This service agreement may be terminated by either party with twenty-four hours' notice sent in writing to the other party by email. If Editor terminates the service agreement, then Client shall pay Editor for work done up to the date of termination, and, if termination occurs before [date], refund the remainder, if any, of the first installment. If Client terminates the service agreement, Editor retains the initial installment and, if termination takes place on or after [date], Client shall also pay Editor for work done up to the date of termination.

10. Warranties

The manuscript will need to be proofread before final publication. Editor makes no representations as to the publishability or profitability of the edited manuscript. Editor will not fact-check the unedited manuscript and does not vouch for the accuracy of facts written by Client **[unless fact checking is part of the contract]**.

Certain aspects of editing are subjective (e.g., rewording for clarity, optional word use). Clients may choose to accept none, some, or all of Editor's editorial changes and/or suggestions. Client's decision to decline some or all editorial changes or suggestions does not constitute nonperformance on the part of Editor and does not entitle Client to a whole or partial refund. Editor strives for perfection but cannot guarantee it.

Editor does not deliver incomplete manuscripts.

11. Acknowledgments

Any acknowledgment in the finished manuscript, if any, must be done with Editor's permission.

12. Copyright of Edited Manuscript

Karin Cather Editorial Services LLC retains sole copyright in the edited manuscript, and grants no license for its use, until Client pays Editor in full as described in this service agreement, at which time said copyright interest will be released in full and transferred to the Client.

13. Indemnity

While Editor will make every effort to bring questionable material to the attention of Client, Client agrees to indemnify and save harmless Editor from any and all claims or demands alleging libel, copyright infringement, portraying a person or corporation in a false light, intentional infliction of emotional distress, or any other cause of action alleged to have been committed by Client in creating or publishing the manuscript. Client agrees that Editor is not responsible for Client's attorney's fees in defending any action brought by third parties as described in this paragraph.

Editor does not have an attorney–client relationship with Client. Editor's work on the manuscript does not constitute legal advice.

14. Severability

The invalidity or unenforceability of any provisions of this service agreement shall not affect the validity or enforceability of any other provision of this service agreement, which shall remain in full force and effect.

15. Applicable laws and jurisdiction

The terms of this service agreement shall be interpreted according to the laws of the state of Arizona and venue and jurisdiction in the event of any dispute arising from this service agreement shall be in the court having jurisdiction in the state of Arizona.

16. Changes.

This service agreement may be changed only by written agreement between the Editor and the Client.

SAMPLE #2: DICK'S TEMPLATE

Statement of Work

Consultant contact

Dick Margulis
Dick Margulis Creative Services
284 West Elm Street
New Haven CT 06515
www.dmargulis.com
dick@dmargulis.com
203-389-4413 (office)
203-464-3199 (cell)

Client contact

NAME
STREET
CITY ST 00000
URL
EMAIL
PHONE 1
PHONE 2

Agreement date

dd mmmm yyyy

Overview

NAME ("client") is the author of SHORT DESCRIPTION, with the working title *WORKING TITLE*. The {professionally edited | final draft} manuscript is approximately 000,000 words long. The book will include NUMBER AND TYPE OF IMAGES. The book {will | will not} have an index.

The client plans to establish a publishing imprint and market the book primarily through BRIEF DESCRIPTION OF MARKETING CHANNELS. The book will be produced as a SPECIFY PRINT FORMAT and as an e-book [if that's the case].

The client wishes to engage Dick Margulis Creative Services ("consultant") for the services described below.

Services

The work to be performed consists of the following services, each of which will commence only after written authorization by client.

Developmental editing
The purpose of development editing in fiction is to help the author construct a compelling plot arc, develop three-dimensional characters, and ensure that dialogue is naturalistic and that the narrative is engaging. THIS DESCRIPTION VARIES FOR DIFFERENT CATEGORIES AND IS SOMETIMES CUSTOMIZED TO THE PARTICULAR MANUSCRIPT.

Line editing
The purpose of line editing is to shape the prose at the paragraph and sentence level to ensure that it reads well.

Copyediting
The purpose of copyediting is to correct errors and inconsistencies in grammar, spelling, punctuation, usage, and style.

Fact checking
Routine and simple fact checking is part of the copyediting process and is not charged separately. Fact checking requiring a separate research effort incurs hourly charges as out-of-scope work.

Markup
The manuscript must be marked up to indicate different categories of text (such as body text, chapter titles, and subheadings), in order to prepare it for composition.

Legal and permissions
Legal review of the manuscript, if needed and authorized by the client, and permissions editing, if needed and authorized by the client, are outsourced to specialists. {Neither service | Legal review | permissions editing} is expected to be needed for this book.

Editing process
All appropriate levels of edit will proceed simultaneously to the extent possible. The consultant will use the Track Changes feature of Microsoft Word, showing all changes. The consultant will use the Comments feature to insert author queries. The client will review all proposed changes, mark those with which {he | she} disagrees or on which {he | she} has questions, and respond to all queries. The consultant will implement all agreed changes. This will conclude a single round of editing.

Editing is charged based on a standard editorial page of 250 words. Words are counted using Microsoft Word's built-in tool.

Interior book design
The design of the book interior encompasses the selection of paper type, page size, margins, typefaces and sizes; and the detailed speci-

fication of typographic parameters and the arrangement of elements on the page.

Design is an iterative process. The consultant will propose one or more candidate designs; the client will provide feedback to help guide the consultant through one or more rounds of revision until both are entirely satisfied with the results. There is no limit to the number of rounds of design revision. However, the design must be approved and final before composition can commence; thus there are practical time constraints on the process.

Design is an economic activity: the choices made affect the cost of composition and the cost of printing and binding. The consultant will advise the client regarding the implications of alternate choices.

The interior design charge is a flat fee.

Composition

Composition consists of importing the edited, marked up manuscript into a typesetting program and applying the approved design to it. The compositor's art includes careful adjustment of typographic elements to achieve an aesthetically pleasing result consistent with commercial composition standards; and the use of proper typographic glyphs for all punctuation, special characters, and foreign alphabets. Composition pricing varies between straight matter (body text, subheadings, extracts) and difficult matter (frontmatter, backmatter, footnotes, captions, chapter openings, sidebars, ordinary tables), and custom artwork (complex tables, charts, diagrams, and other illustrations). Composition also includes the preparation and insertion of furnished images.

Changes made by the client after pages are composed are author's alterations (AAs). They are charged per sentence affected. Changes that cause type to move from one page to another, resulting in a need for layout adjustment, also incur charges for such adjustments. Corrections resulting from composition errors are printer's errors (PEs) and are not charged.

Composition is charged per finished book page (fbp). Proofreading is charged either per fbp or per editorial page (word count), depending on the proofreader contracted with.

Proofreading
Proofreading is the checking of typeset pages for composition errors. Proofreading also includes a cold read, meaning the proofreader looks for places where the copyeditor has missed an error that should be fixed. Proofreading is outsourced to a professional proofreader upon authorization by the client.

Indexing
A professional indexer will be engaged upon authorization by the client. The index is constructed after pages are typeset, typically in parallel with proofreading. The index manuscript is offered to the client for review and approval. The final version is typeset and checked by the indexer before files are released for printing.

Cover design and production
Cover design consists of the selection of binding features and materials; the selection of artwork and the typographic design of front cover, back cover, and spine; and the editing and preparation of cover copy.

Cover design is an iterative process. The consultant will propose one or more candidate designs; the client will provide feedback to help guide the consultant through one or more rounds of revision until both are entirely satisfied with the results. There is no limit to the number of rounds of design revision. However, the design must be approved and final before printing can commence; thus there are practical time constraints on the process.

Cover design is an economic activity: the choices made affect the cost of design, printing and binding. The consultant will advise the client regarding the implications of alternate choices.

Cover design and production charges are flat fees based on the type of binding selected and do not include the cost of purchased or licensed artwork, which is charged as an expense.

E-book preparation
After page composition of the print book, a slightly modified version of the finished layout files as prepared by the consultant will be pro-

vided to a conversion service for conversion to Kindle-compatible and ePub formats suitable for uploading to e-book retailer websites.

Project management

1. (optional clerical tasks that the client can perform): The consultant will assist the client in setting up a publishing imprint with Bowker, Inc.; and obtaining a block of ISBNs. The consultant will obtain a Library of Congress Control Number (LCCN) for the book. The consultant will enter the book in the Books in Print database and will register the book's U.S. copyright in the name of the author. The consultant will prepare copy for the copyright page.
2. The consultant will advise on the selection of outside vendors, will engage them as authorized by the client, and will coordinate their efforts. Outside vendors may include a proofreader, an indexer, one or more book manufacturers, an e-book conversion and distribution service, a book fulfillment service, and other specialists as required.

    The client will have the opportunity to review the work of outside vendors. For example, the client may review changes suggested by the proofreader (AAs) and authorize or not authorize them on an individual basis.
3. An included service consists of up to one hour of telephone consultation and up to one hour of routine email correspondence. Client-initiated phone calls and correspondence in excess of those limits are billed as work outside of scope.
4. The consultant will be available to support the client's marketing efforts, with specific projects to be quoted and contracted separately, outside the scope of this agreement. Such projects may include writing, editing, design, and production of marketing collateral, website updates, or other activities in support of the client's plan.

Furnished materials

DESCRIBE AS NEEDED

Schedule

LIST MILESTONES, WHO IS RESPONSIBLE, EXPECTED DATES

Deliverables

Deliverables will consist of PDF files (of pages and cover for printing). Native design and layout application files remain the property of the consultant; they can be placed in an escrow account at the client's expense, to ensure future availability in the event the consultant goes out of business. Finished books will be delivered by the manufacturer to location or locations specified by the client.

Termination

The client may terminate this agreement for any reason upon ten days' written notice and fair compensation for work performed to date. Consultant must cease all work immediately upon notification. Any deposit paid is nonrefundable.

The consultant may terminate this agreement for any reason upon the refund of any unearned deposit and delivery of work completed to date.

Client and consultant agree that the purpose of this agreement is to assign responsibilities and to align expectations. They further agree that the amount of money at stake is insufficient to justify involving legal counsel or any form of formal dispute resolution (including mediation, arbitration, or lawsuit) and that therefore the sole remedy in the event of a misunderstanding that cannot be resolved through good-faith negotiation is termination under this section.

Assumptions

- This proposal is valid for thirty days from the cover date and may be withdrawn or modified if not accepted within that period.

- Contents of this proposal are confidential and may not be shared with any party other than the client's legal and business advisers.
- The client is the author and sole owner of all rights in the book's text.
- The client asserts the right to include any images furnished for use in the book.
- The client will respond in a timely manner to queries from the consultant as the work progresses, with unambiguous and final answers.
- The client acknowledges that after the client approves final corrections, any residual errors are the client's responsibility.
- The client asserts that the manuscript is an original work and does not contain any plagiarized material and that the client's use of any previously published material is done with the written permission of its copyright owner or else within the doctrine of fair use.
- The client holds the consultant harmless against any charges of libel, invasion of privacy, plagiarism, or copyright infringement and indemnifies the consultant against any costs incurred in defending against such charges.
- The consultant asserts that all designs are original work and that no third-party artwork will be incorporated into the finished book unless it is in the public domain or the client has secured a license for its use.
- The client will provide such information as is needed to complete third-party transactions, if any (such as providing a credit card number for vendors requiring that information).
- The quoted price includes work as described above. Out-of-scope work will incur hourly charges.
- The client accepts responsibility for all client-approved incidental expenses and third-party charges, including but not limited to: professional proofreading, professional indexing, book manufacturing, book logistics, and e-book conversion and distribution services; licensing of artwork or special fonts selected by client; and incidental desktop printing and express charges

associated with shipping final files to a printer, checking page proofs, etc.
- The client agrees to execute any needed licensing agreements for artwork used and any needed credit applications and purchase contracts for printing, binding, delivery, warehousing, and distribution of finished books.
- The client agrees that the consultant will be credited for book design and composition on the copyright page of this and any future editions making use of his work, with such credit also to include the consultant's business URL so long as it remains valid.
- The client agrees to furnish the consultant with seven complimentary copies of the best printed edition of the book for distribution to the proofreader (one, signed by the author); the indexer (one, signed by the author); the consultant (two, one of them signed by the author); and the Library of Congress (two for the Copyright Office and one for the LCCN office) in a timely manner.
- The client agrees that the consultant will have the opportunity to review any mention of the consultant in the book's acknowledgments and to accept any such mention as is, correct it if it contains errors, or decline to be mentioned, at the consultant's sole discretion.
- The client will keep track of total sales and will inform the consultant of the number of copies sold upon request, such requests to occur no more than twice during the year after publication and once per year thereafter, with this provision expiring three years from publication date.

Risks

- To the extent the work does not progress in accordance with assumptions, final delivery may be delayed, potentially affecting availability on the desired date.

- To the extent that furnished materials are inconsistent with stated requirements, additional charges may apply.
- Despite the best efforts of all parties, the finished book may contain a small number of residual errors. Perfection is never promised and rarely achieved.
- Despite the best efforts of client and consultant, the book may not succeed in the marketplace, and a financial loss to the client may result.

Pricing

Note that pricing is à la carte for services the client selects.

Editing, comprehensive, per 250 words
    First round $ 0.00
    Second and subsequent rounds, if authorized   0.00
Interior book design $ 000.00
Composition
    Straight matter per finished book page (fbp)   0.00
    Difficult matter, per fbp   0.00
    Image scanning, each   0.00
    Routine image preparation and insertion, each   0.00
    Custom artwork, per hour   000.00
    AAs, each   0.00
Cover design and production,
    Softcover, standard   000.00
    Other options available (inquire)
E-book preparation
    Base charge   000.00
    Additional per image   0.00
Project management
    Item 1 (optional clerical tasks)   000.00
    Item 2 (administrative fee added to vendor invoices)
    All vendors except book manufacturers   00% of cost

Book manufacturers	0% of cost
Item 4 to be covered by separate agreements	
Additional work outside of scope, per hour	000.00

Terms

A deposit of $0,000 is due with signed agreement. Invoices for work completed are due when rendered. Amounts over 30 days are subject to a finance charge of 1.5% per month (18% annual percentage rate). Amounts over 90 days are subject to collection, with reasonable collection costs to be paid by the client. The consultant retains a copyright interest in the edited book that will be relinquished automatically upon receipt of final payment.

AGREED

[CLIENT FIRM IF ANY]   Dick Margulis Creative Services

_____   _____
CLIENT NAME   Dick Margulis

_____   _____
Date   Date

Printed in Great Britain
by Amazon